# juices and
# smoothies

by Jan Castorina, Dimitra Stais
and Tracy Rutherford

TUTTLE PUBLISHING
Tokyo • Rutland, Vermont • Singapore

Published by Tuttle Publishing, an imprint of Periplus
Editions, with editorial offices at 130 Joo Seng Road,
#06-01, Singapore 368357, and 364 Innovation Drive,
North Clarendon, VT 05759, USA.

ISBN 10: 0-8048-3867-4
ISBN 13: 978-0-8048-3867-2
Printed in Malaysia

Distributed by
**North America, Latin America and Europe**
Tuttle Publishing, 364 Innovation Drive,
North Clarendon, VT 05759-9436.
Tel: (802) 773-8930  Fax: (802) 773-6993
Email: info@tuttlepublishing.com
www.tuttlepublishing.com

**Japan**
Tuttle Publishing, Yaekari Building 3F,
5-4-12 Osaki, Shinagawa-ku, Tokyo 141-0032.
Tel: (03) 5437-0171  Fax: (03) 5437-0755
Email: tuttle-sales@gol.com

**Asia Pacific**
Berkeley Books Pte Ltd.
130 Joo Seng Road #06-01
Singapore 368357.
Tel: (65) 6280-1330  Fax: (65) 6280-6290
Email: inquiries@periplus.com.sg
www.periplus.com

10 09 08 07
5 4 3 2 1

TUTTLE PUBLISHING® is a registered trademark of Tuttle Publishing,
a division of Periplus Editions (HK) Ltd.

# Contents

# Ingredient Glossary

**Carob powder** is the finely ground roasted carob pod. It is similar in appearance, flavor and texture to cocoa powder, and is often used as a substitute. It is nutritious and caffeine free.

**Custard apples**, also known as cherimoyas, are large, vaguely heart-shaped fruits with knobbly, apple green skin and flesh that is a cross between bananas and mangoes in flavor. A ripe custard apple may have a few dark spots on the skin; more than this, and the fruit is overripe. When ripe, it will give slightly to a gentle squeezeThe cream-colored flesh contains hard black seeds. To prepare a custard apple, cut it in half and scoop out the flesh, discarding the seeds. The seeds can hide in the dense flesh, so make sure you remove them all. Custard apples contain vitamin C and some minerals, such as calcium and iron.

**Fig** ranges from very pale green, to red and green, to deep purple-brown, depending on the variety. The flesh is pinkish red to creamy yellow and has many tiny edible seeds. A ripe fig yields to gentle pressure and, because it is highly perishable, should be eaten as soon as possible. Figs are a good source of calcium and potassium, dietary fiber and vitamins A, B and C.

**Flaxseed** is also known as linseed. This fruit is a good source of omega-3 fatty acids, which have many health benefits, including the prevention of heart disease.

**Kiwifruit** has a dull, slightly fuzzy skin which hides a vibrant green interior with a paler core surrounded by tiny edible black seeds. A ripe kiwifruit gives slightly to gentle pressure. If very soft, it is overripe and will have an unpleasant fermented taste. Very rich in vitamin C, kiwifruit also contains vitamin E. See page 9 for preparation.

**Passion fruit** is a round fruit with leathery, dark purple skin, which when opened reveals juicy yellow pulp containing many small, black edible seeds. The smooth skin becomes wrinkled over time. If the fruit still feels heavy, it is usable, but very wrinkled fruit may be too old and the pulp inside will be dried out. Passion fruit is a good source of vitamins A and C. See page 8 for preparation.

The Hachiya **persimmon** is the best variety for use in blended drinks. It is astringent and unpleasant when under-ripe but is sweet and juicy when ripe, by which time it is an intense orange-red. Ripe Hachiyas are extremely soft and should be handled with great care to avoid puncturing or bruising. To prepare a persimmon, cut in half and scoop out the pulpy flesh, discarding any seeds. High in vitamin A, this fruit also contains calcium, thiamin, potassium and iron.

**Pomegranate** is a round fruit with tough, pinkish red skin. Inside there is minimal pulp, along with tough membranes and many seeds. The gorgeous red juice is appreciated for its tart flavor. The seeds are often used as a garnish on sweet and savory dishes. Pomegranates are a good source of vitamin C. See page 9 for preparation.

**Protein whey powder** is a dairy by-product which is added to drinks as a dietary supplement, to increase protein intake.

**Red papaya** is similar to the yellow-skinned, yellow-fleshed papaya, but smaller and has red-orange flesh. This variety is similarly rich in beta-carotene and also contains the carotenoid lycopene, which may be proven to be an even more powerful antioxidant.

**Semi-dry dates** have a higher water content than dried dates and are therefore softer in texture. High in natural sugar, the sweet, sticky flesh is very nutritious, containing minerals such as calcium, iron, potassium and magnesium, as well as dietary fiber. Dates have a single pit, which is easy

to remove. Dates are occasionally available pitted.

**Spirulina** is a natural food supplement made from *spirulina,* a type of blue green algae. It is taken as a rich source of protein, vitamins, minerals and a poweful antioxidant. Spirulina is sold in the form of a powder, tablet or capsule, and is often added to health tonics.

**Tofu** is a curd made by adding a setting agent to soy milk. It can be either firm or soft (silken). The soft variety is required for drink recipes, to give a smooth consistency.

**Tamarillo** is an oval fruit with a smooth, thick, deep red or yellow-orange skin, depending on the variety. The flesh is orange and contains small edible black seeds. Soft to touch when ripe, tamarillos must be peeled to remove the bitter skin. The flesh has a sharp, tangy flavor that is pleasantly sweet and sour. Tamarillos are a good source of potassium and vitamin A.

# Preparing Fruits

**Preparing Passion Fruits**

**1** Pierce the thick skin with a knife, then slice the fruit in half. Cutting the skin with a sawing motion can be dangerous, as the knife could slip.

**2** Scoop the pulp out of the skin with a small spoon.

**Preparing Mangoes**

**1** The flat pit runs lengthwise through the fruit, roughly through the center third. Cut the flesh from either side of the pit in one piece, running the knife as close to the pit as possible.

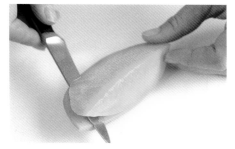

**2** Cut each mango piece in half lengthwise, then run the knife between the peel and the flesh to remove as much flesh as possible. Cut any remaining flesh from the pit.

**Preparing Avocados**

**1** Cut through the avocado lengthwise and all the way around the pit. Gently twist the halves in opposite directions, then pull apart. The pit will remain in one half.

**2** Sharply strike the pit with the blade of a knife, then twist the knife to lift out the pit.

### Preparing Tamarillos

**1** To peel soft fruits such as peaches, apricots, plums or tamarillos (pictured), cut a small X in the bottom of each fruit. Cover with boiling water and let stand for 1 minute. The skin should curl away at the X. Drain and rinse under cold running water.

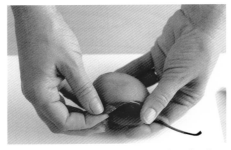

**2** When the fruit is cool enough to handle, slip the skin off with your fingers.

### Preparing Peaches

**1** Cut around the fruit deep enough just to touch the pit with the knife.

**2** Gently twist the halves in opposite directions to release them from the pit. Carefully pull out the pit with your fingers or cut out with a small knife.

### Peeling Kiwifruit

Slice the ends off the fruit with a small, sharp knife. Stand the fruit upright and cut off the skin, working your way around the fruit.

### Juicing Pomegranates

Cut the fruit in half crosswise. Use a citrus reamer with a shallow bowl to extract and collect the juice. Press it against the reamer. Watch out for splashing juice, which will stain fabric. If the juice contains bits of seeds or white membrane, pass it through a fine-mesh strainer.

# Extraction Methods

To make the drinks in this book, you will need a blender, juice extractor and citrus juicer. The blender is used to make fruit smoothies and drinks from soft fruits such as bananas, persimmons and passion fruits. To make juice from hard fruits and vegetables, you will need a juice extractor. Citrus fruits can be juiced easily with any kind of citrus juicer.

**Blenders:** There are many blenders available, varying in size and power. When choosing one, check the motor size, how easy it is to clean and reassemble, and whether it has more than one speed. Some come with a handy grinder for coffee beans or for nuts and seeds. Although blenders range in price, you should invest in a good-quality one that will last for years without problems.

**Juice extractors:** If you intend to make juices a regular part of your life, it is worth investing in a good-quality juice extractor. Make sure you shop around and ask about the features of each machine: how it operates, what style it is, how it is cleaned, the size of the motor and, of course, the price. All these points will help you determine which kind to purchase. The following are the three main types of juice extractors, as determined by the kind of motor that powers them.

    **Centrifugal extractors:** This type of extractor finely grates food and uses centrifugal force to expel the extracted juice into a container. These extractors either allow the pulp to accumulate within the machine's container or expel the pulp into another container. The benefit of the latter type is that you don't have to stop and empty out the pulp quite as often. A centrifugal motor tends to add oxygen to juices, which can decrease their keeping time as oxygen destroys certain vitamins. If you have this style of extractor, always drink your juices immediately to gain the most nutrients.

    **Masticating extractors:** More expensive than the centrifugal type, the masticating extractor finely grates the food and then "chews" it to make even finer particles. It then presses the pulp to extract the juices, expelling the pulp after the juice is extracted. It doesn't incorporate oxygen into the juices, so it provides high-quality juice which will keep for a day in a refrigerator.

    **Hydraulic press extractors:** The most expensive and efficient type, this machine grates food, then crushes it with revolving cutters. The pulp is put under tremendous pressure to extract all the juice, leaving a very dry pulp. This extractor makes juice with the highest amount of nutrients and doesn't incorporate oxygen during the process. Juices made with this type of extractor can be stored in airtight containers in the refrigerator for a day or two.

**Citrus juicers:** These are available in a wide variety, from simple manual juicers to electric ones. They all do more or less the same job, and the type you purchase will depend on your taste and budget.

# Lemon Carrot Orange Juice

A juice for sufferers of chronic fatigue syndrome—the lemon stimulates gallbladder and liver functions while the carrot helps boost the immune system.

1 orange, peeled, deseeded and
   sliced
$1/_2$ lemon, peeled and sliced
2 medium carrots, sliced

In a juice extractor, process all the ingredients until well blended. Drink immediately.

Serves 1
Makes about 1 cup (250 ml)

# Blackcurrant Orange Egg-flip

This drink is full of excellent nutrients for the chronically ill. It provides the protein from eggs and milk, flavonoids from currants and B vitamins from yeast.

$3/_4$ cup (180 ml) milk or fortified
   soy milk, chilled
$3/_4$ cup (100 g) frozen blackcur-
   rants or other berries, thawed
1 egg
$1/_4$ cup (60 ml) water
2 teaspoons honey, or to taste
1 teaspoon grated orange zest
$1/_2$ teaspoon brewer's yeast

In a blender, combine all the ingredients and process until smooth.

Serves 1
Makes about $1^1/_4$ cups (300 ml)

# Pineapple Carrot Broccoli Immune Enhancer

For those with HIV or a chronic viral illness, it is very important to enhance the immune function. Carotenes and vitamin C help achieve this and are plentiful in this drink. Zinc can also benefit, so sunflower and pumpkin seeds should be eaten daily for their zinc content.

$1/_4$ fresh medium pineapple,
   peeled, cored and sliced
1 medium carrot, sliced
1 cup (125 g) chopped broccoli

Process all the ingredients in a juice extractor until smooth. Drink immediately.

Serves 1
Makes about $1^1/_4$ cups (300 ml)

# Pineapple Ginger Pick-me-up

This is a good drink to have while working or studying, as the enzymes in the pineapple help to keep you alert and aid concentration.

$3/4$ in (2 cm) fresh ginger root, peeled and sliced
$1/2$ fresh medium pineapple, peeled, cored and sliced
$1/2$ teaspoon minced fresh mint

In a juice extractor, process the ginger and pineapple until smooth, then stir in the mint.

Serves 1
Makes about 1 cup (250 ml)

# Fast Breakfast Drink

A nutritious breakfast that can be made in a flash, this drink provides many essential nutrients such as carbohydrate, protein, vitamins, folate, zinc and magnesium. The yogurt provides the friendly bacteria, which help to boost immunity.

1 cup (250 ml) milk or fortified soy milk, chilled
$1/4$ cup (60 ml) natural yogurt
4 oz (125 g) strawberries
2 medium passion fruits, halved and flesh scooped from peel
2 teaspoons wheat germ
2 teaspoons honey or sugar

Process all the ingredients in a blender until smooth. Serve immediately.

Serves 2
Makes about $2^1/2$ cups (625 ml)

# Carrot Tomato Cucumber Lifter

A good drink to have when you have to work late. The basil helps concentration and aids digestion. Tomato juice provides nutrients that help to stimulate blood circulation, and cucumber helps you to stay alert.

2 medium carrots, chilled and sliced
1 small tomato, chilled and sliced
1 small cucumber, chilled and sliced
5–6 large fresh basil leaves, minced

In a juice extractor, process the carrot, tomato and cucumber until smooth and well blended. Pour into a glass, stir in the basil and drink immediately.

Serves 1
Makes about $1^1/4$ cups (300 ml)

# Hot Lemon Drink

This is an excellent drink when you have a cold or flu, or feel one coming on. The lemon provides vitamin C, the ginger and chili powder help to clear the sinuses, and the honey soothes a sore throat. When making this drink for a child, dilute it with more hot water and reduce or omit the chili powder.

$3/4$ cup (180 ml) boiling water
1 teaspoon grated lemon zest
$1/4$ cup (60 ml) fresh lemon juice
1 teaspoon grated fresh ginger root
3 teaspoons honey, or to taste
Pinch of chili powder

In a mug, combine all the ingredients and stir well. Serve hot.

Serves 1
Makes about 1 cup (250 ml)

# Citrus Cold and Flu Fighter

Onion and garlic are excellent expectorants and help to break up congestion, and garlic is a strong natural antibiotic. The citrus fruits provide vitamin C to help boost the immune system, and honey soothes a sore throat.

1 small clove garlic
$1/8$ red onion, sliced
$1/2$ lemon, peeled and sliced
1 orange, peeled and sliced
$1/2$ teaspoon honey, or to taste

In a juice extractor, process the garlic, onion, lemon and orange. Add the honey and whisk until well combined.

Serves 1
Makes about $2/3$ cup (160 ml)

# Smooth Orange Healer

After you have had a virus, you need lots of nutrients to boost your immune system. This drink contains vitamin C, beta-carotene, bioflavonoids, a natural antibiotic from the garlic, B vitamins from the yeast and more.

1 clove garlic
$3/4$ cup (20 g) fresh parsley sprigs
8 oz (250 g) papaya, peeled, deseeded and sliced
1 orange, peeled and sliced
$1/2$ teaspoon brewer's yeast

In a juice extractor, process the garlic, then the parsley, papaya and orange. Whisk in the yeast, if using.

Serves 1
Makes about 1 cup (250 ml)

# Refreshing Grapefruit Lifter

Winter can make you feel a bit blue, but this fresh-tasting drink will help to lift
your spirits, improve your digestion and boost your immune system with
a good hit of vitamin C. Fennel and ginger also help to clear the sinuses.

$3/4$ in (2 cm) fresh ginger root,
  peeled and sliced
1 medium fennel bulb, sliced
$1/2$ medium apple, sliced
$1^1/_2$ grapefruits (about 350 g),
  peeled and sliced

In a juice extractor, process all the ingredients until
smooth.

Serves 1
Makes about 1 cup (250 ml)

# Lemon Balm Pineapple Drink

This is a lovely drink to have when you are about to travel. Pineapple helps
to keep you alert, lemon balm reduces pre-travel stress,
and ginger helps to prevent motion sickness.

1 lemon balm tea bag
$1/4$ cup (60 ml) boiling water
$3/4$ in (2 cm) fresh ginger root,
  peeled and sliced
$1/4$ fresh medium pineapple,
  peeled, cored and sliced

**1** Place the tea bag in a mug and add the hot water. Let
the mixture steep for 15 minutes, then remove the tea bag.
**2** In a juice extractor, process the ginger and pineapple
until smooth. Pour in the tea and whisk well.

Serves 1
Makes about 1 cup (250 ml)

# Carrot Bell Pepper Lime Juice

This juice provides antioxidants—beta-carotene, flavonoids and vitamin C—
which reduce the free-radical activity that can promote cancer growth.

2 medium carrots, sliced
$1/2$ large red bell pepper, deseeded
  and sliced
Finely grated zest and fresh juice
  of 1 lime

In a juice extractor, process the carrot and bell pepper
until smooth. Combine with the lime zest and juice, and
mix well.

Serves 1
Makes about $1^1/_4$ cups (300 ml)

# Super Orange Booster

Full of vitamin C, folate and beta-carotene, this drink helps to boost immune functions and would be good to take before having surgery. It's a deliciously sweet drink. The lemon balm helps to promote calmness and serenity.

$^1/_2$ mango, peeled and pitted
1 orange, peeled, deseeded and sliced
1 carrot, sliced
$^1/_2$ teaspoon finely chopped fresh lemon balm

In a juice extractor, process the mango, orange and carrot until smooth, then whisk in the lemon balm.

Serves 1
Makes about 1 cup (250 ml)

# Chlorophyll Booster

When you are chronically ill, your system can often do with a gentle cleanse and some good-quality nutrients. This drink provides plenty of chlorophyll, which is an excellent internal cleanser, and folate, which can assist with depression. The spirulina provides excellent nutrients like protein, vitamin B12 and natural iron.

2 large apples, sliced
$^3/_4$ cup (100 g) chopped broccoli
$^1/_2$–1 teaspoon spirulina, or to taste

In a juice extractor, process the apple and broccoli until smooth. Whisk in the spirulina and drink at once.

Serves 1
Makes about $1^1/_4$ cups (300 ml)

# Pear Licorice Orange Drink

This juice is an anti-inflammatory drink that combines the anti-allergy and inflammation-reducing qualities of licorice with orange zest for its natural bioflavonoids. Pear juice, supplies some vitamin C.

2 teaspoons chopped dried licorice root
$^1/_4$ cup (60 ml) boiling water
1 large pear, cut into wedges
1 teaspoon finely grated orange zest

1 In a small bowl, soak the licorice in the boiling water, covered, for 10 minutes. Strain and reserve the liquid.
2 Process the pear in a juice extractor until smooth than combine well with the licorice liquid and orange zest .

Serves 1
Makes about 1 cup (250 ml)

# Warm Grapefruit Drink

This old but effective remedy should be drunk on an empty stomach first thing in the morning. The bitter citrus juice promotes gallbladder functions, which in turn helps stimulate the digestive system and prevents constipation.

1 grapefruit or lemon
$1/_2$ cup (125 ml) hot water

Serves 1
Makes about $1^1/_4$ cups (300 ml) grapefruit drink, or $3/_4$ cup (180 ml) lemon drink

Squeeze the juice from the grapefruit or lemon using a citrus juicer, or peel and chop the grapefruit or lemon into small pieces and process in a juice extractor. Pour into a cup and whisk in the hot water. Drink while warm.

# Apple Pear Beet Juice

For a spring cleaning any time of the year, one day a week eat only light foods such as vegetables, rice and fruit, and drink cleansing juices. The beet increases liver activities, while the psyllium absorbs any toxins released and aids in their elimination.

1 medium apple, sliced
1 medium pear, sliced
$1/_2$ large beetroot, sliced
2 teaspoons psyllium husks

In a juice extractor, process the apple, pear and beetroot until smooth. Whisk in the psyllium and drink instantly.

Serves 1
Makes about $1^1/_4$ cups (300 ml)

# Orange Apricot Whip

If you have given up smoking, drink this regularly to encourage the repair of lung tissue. The beta-carotene in the apricots is converted to vitamin A and helps in the maintenance of mucous membranes; an antioxidant. It also absorbs free radicals. Vitamin C and E (from the orange and wheat germ oil respectively), also antioxidants, are often depleted in those who smoke.

5 oz (150 g) canned apricots, drained
$3/_4$ cup (180 ml) fresh orange juice
1 teaspoon grated fresh ginger root
$1/_2$ teaspoon wheat germ oil

Process all the ingredients in a blender until smooth and well combined.

Serves 1–2    Makes about $1^1/_2$ cups (375 ml)

# Clean Green Juice

This green drink is rich in chlorophyll, an excellent body cleanser, and contains nutrients such as folate, carotene and potassium, all essential for good health.

5 small spinach leaves
1 medium green bell pepper, deseeded and sliced
1 stalk celery with leaves, sliced
2 large lettuce leaves

In a juice extractor, process the spinach leaves, then the bell pepper, celery and lettuce until well combined.

Serves 1
Makes about 1 cup (250 ml)

# Cucumber Beet Cocktail

Beetroot is often used for cleansing and to relieve constipation. Because it can have quite a strong effect on the body, in this drink, we have diluted it with cucumber, an excellent cleanser and soda water.

$1/_2$ medium beetroot, sliced
1 small cucumber, sliced
$1^1/_2$ cups (375 ml) soda water
Squeeze of fresh lime juice

In a juice extractor, process the beetroot and cucumber until smooth. Stir in the soda water and lime juice.

Serves 2
Makes about 2 cups (500 ml)

# Orange Pepper Turmeric Detoxifier

This drink helps to detoxify any accumulation of chemical toxins which cause stress on the body. Turmeric has liver-protective qualities and the dandelion to improves the functional capacity of the liver. Psyllium absorbs and helps to eliminatetoxins from the body, while the orange juice and pepper provide vitamin C and carotenes.

1 teaspoon roasted dandelion root
$1/_4$ cup (60 ml) boiling water
1 orange, peeled, deseeded and sliced
$1/_2$ large red bell pepper, deseeded and sliced
1 in (3 cm) fresh turmeric, peeled and sliced
2 teaspoons psyllium husks

1 In a large mug, combine the dandelion root and boiling water. Cover and let the mixture steep for 10 minutes. Strain and reserve the liquid, then let it cool.
2 In a juice extractor, process the orange, bell pepper and turmeric until smooth. Add to the dandelion tea, whisk in the psyllium and drink immediately.

Serves 1
Makes about $1^1/_4$ cups (300 ml)

# Clear-skin Strawberry Juice

A juice for teenagers, it helps to cleanse the skin from the inside and reduces pimple outbreaks. The strawberries provide vitamin C, and the cucumber is an excellent natural diuretic and internal cleanser.

8 oz (250 g) fresh or thawed
  strawberries
1 small cucumber, sliced

In a juice extractor, process the strawberries and cucumber until smooth.

Serves 1
Makes about 1 cup (250 ml)

# Kiwi Apple Juice

This is an all-round healthy drink for the whole family. It contains vitamin C, some soluble fiber from the pectin in the apples, and enzymes that aid digestion.

4 large kiwifruit, peeled and
  sliced
4 large green apples, sliced

Process all the ingredients in a juice extractor until well blended.

Serves 1
Makes about $1^1/_4$ cups (300 ml)

# Strawberry Pineapple Whip

A drink high in vitamin C for kids to have after school or for breakfast. It contains enzymes that help with digestion and carbohydrates for energy, while strawberries promote clear skin.

4 oz (125 g) fresh or thawed
  strawberries
$1/_2$ medium pear, sliced
$1/_4$ fresh medium pineapple,
  peeled, cored and sliced
1 orange, peeled, deseeded and
  sliced

In a juice extractor, process the strawberries, then the pear, pineapple and orange until well blended.

Serves 2
Makes about 2 cups (500 ml)

# Orange Carrot Papaya Juice

If your children dislike eating vegetables, serve them this delicious juice. The
carrot provides essential beta-carotene, orange supplies vitamin C
and papaya adds beta-carotene and enzymes that aid digestion.

1 papaya (about 400 g), peeled,
  deseeded and sliced
1 orange, peeled and sliced
1 carrot, sliced

Process all the ingredients in a juice extractor.

Serves 1–2 (depending on age)
Makes about 1$^1$/$_2$ cups (375 ml)

# Persimmon or Mango Breakfast Drink

This hearty drink supplies many essential nutrients. Persimmons and mangoes are
rich in beta-carotene, sunflower seeds are rich in essential fatty acids, and milk,
soy milk and yogurt provide calcium. Wheat germ contributes fiber and vitamin E.

7 oz (200 g) chopped ripe persimmons or mangoes
1 cup (250 ml) milk or fortified
  soy milk
$^1$/$_2$ cup (125 g) natural yogurt
1 passion fruit, halved, pulp removed
3 teaspoons wheat germ
3 teaspoons sunflower seed kernels
$^1$/$_3$ cup (90 ml) water

Process all the ingredients in a blender until smooth.
Add a little water if necessary to reach a drinkable
consistency.

Serves 3
Makes about 3 cups (750 ml)

# Calming Prune Chamomile Tea

Try this when you need to relax. Chamomile is a calming herb, while prunes
provide pantothenic acid (B5) essential for reducing stress.

1 chamomile tea bag, or 1 teaspoon dried chamomile
$^3$/$_4$ cup (180 ml) boiling water
$^1$/$_2$ cup (125 ml) natural yogurt
6 prunes, pitted
1 teaspoon grated orange zest
1 teaspoon honey

**1** Place the tea bag or chamomile in a cup and add the
boiling water. Let the mixture steep for 10 minutes.
Strain and reserve the tea. Chill the tea.
**2** In a blender, process the tea and all the other ingredients until smooth.

Serves 1    Makes about 1$^1$/$_3$ cups (330 ml)

# Pear Mango Shake

This is a nutritious drink for older people. It contains lots of soluble fiber to help prevent constipation. The wheat germ contributes vitamin E; the milk adds calcium; the yogurt supplies calcium, friendly bacteria, vitamin B12 and folate; and the mango provides beta-carotene, which helps prevent cataracts.

1 cup (100 g) chopped mango
$^3/_4$ cup (180 ml) low-fat milk or
   fortified soy milk
1 teaspoon wheat germ
$^1/_4$ cup (60 ml) natural yogurt
5 oz (150 g) canned pears, drained
Honey or sugar, to taste

Process all the ingredients in a blender until smooth.

Serves 2
Makes about 2 cups (375 ml)

# Pear Apple Pineapple Juice

We recommend this juice for adults, especially the elderly, who may be prone to constipation and arthritis. The pear and apple provides excellent fiber to relieve constipation, while the pineapple contains bromelain, an enzyme that has been shown to reduce the inflammation of arthritis.

$^1/_2$ medium pear, sliced
$^1/_2$ medium apple, sliced
$^1/_2$ fresh medium pineapple,
   peeled, cored and sliced

Process all the ingredients in a juice extractor until smooth.

Serves 1
Makes about 1$^1/_4$ cups (300 ml)

# Orange, Carrot, Guava and Corn Juice

This drink is packed with antioxidants, which are a natural form of anti-aging nutrients for adults.

1 medium carrot, sliced
1 orange, zest grated, peel dis-
   carded, flesh sliced
$^1/_2$ large guava, sliced
$^2/_3$ cup (90 g) fresh or thawed
   corn kernels

Process all the ingredients in a juice extractor until well blended.

Serves 1
Makes about 1 cup (250 ml)

# Pineapple, Celery, Ginger and Watercress Juice

An anti-inflammatory drink. The pineapple, ginger and celery all have anti-inflammatory properties, and the watercress provides some folate, chlorophyll and iron.

$1/_4$ fresh large pineapple, peeled, cored, and sliced
2 stalks celery with leaves, sliced
1 cup (75 g) watercress
$1/_2$ in (1 cm) fresh ginger root, peeled and sliced
1 teaspoon celery seeds, ground

In a juice extractor, process the pineapple, celery, watercress and ginger until smooth, then whisk in the celery seeds, if using.

Serves 1
Makes about $1^1/_4$ cups (300 ml)

# Cucumber, Apple, Turmeric and Ginger Juice

Turmeric and feverfew have anti-inflammatory qualities, and the cucumber and apple contain silica needed for healthy bones and connective tissue. This drink helps to reduce the pain caused by arthritis.

1 small cucumber, sliced
1 medium green apple, sliced
1 in (3 cm) fresh turmeric, peeled and sliced
$1/_2$ in (1 cm) fresh ginger root, peeled, sliced
5 fresh feverfew leaves, minced

In a juice extractor, process the cucumber, apple, turmeric and ginger until smooth, then whisk in the feverfew.

Serves 1
Makes about 1 cup (250 ml)

# Orange Blood Builder

Anemia can be caused by lack of iron, folate or vitamin B12. This drink contains all three nutrients to help maintain healthy blood.

5 dried apricots, finely chopped
$1/_2$ cup (125 ml) water
$3/_4$ cup (180 ml) fresh orange juice
$1/_3$ cup (15 g) chopped parsley
$1/_2$ teaspoon spirulina

1 Combine the apricots and water in a saucepan and bring to boil. Reduce the heat to low, cover and simmer for 15 minutes. Remove from the heat and set aside to cool.
2 Combine the boiled apricots and water with all the other ingredients and process until smooth in a blender.

Serves 1
Makes about 1 cup (250 ml)

# Prune Apple Smoothie

Prunes have long been used to promote elimination,
and black pepper is a stimulant that helps to prevent constipation.

4 pitted prunes (about 60 g)
1 cup (250 ml) water
Pinch of ground black pepper
$^1/_2$ cup (125 ml) fresh apple juice

Serves 1
Makes about $^3/_4$ cup (180 ml)

**1** Bring the prunes and water to a boil in a small pot. Reduce the heat to low, cover and simmer for 10 minutes. Remove from the heat and set aside to cool.
**2** Combine the prunes and water with the remaining ingredients and process in a blender until smooth.

# Celery Root Juice

Celery root and broccoli contain magnesium and calcium—nutrients that help
to prevent leg cramps. The apple lightens the flavor, while the lemon juice
provides vitamin C and prevents the celery root juice from discoloring.

8 oz (250 g) celery root, peeled
  and sliced, or broccoli, chopped
1 medium apple, sliced
$^1/_2$ lemon, peeled and sliced

Process the celery root, then the apple and then the lemon in a juice extractor until smooth.

Serves 1
Makes about 1 cup (250 ml)

# Papaya, Orange, Rose Hip and Cardamom Drink

Cardamom and oregano reduce coughs, while rose hip contains vitamin C.
Papaya contains beta-carotene and soothes a sore throat.

$^1/_2$ teaspoon cardamom seeds
1 rose hip tea bag
1 teaspoon chopped fresh
  oregano leaves
$^1/_4$ cup (60 ml) boiling water
1 ripe papaya (about 380 g),
  peeled, deseeded and sliced
1 orange, peeled, deseeded and
  sliced

**1** Crush the cardamom seeds and place in a cup with the tea bag and oregano. Add the boiling water and allow the mixture to steep for 15 minutes. Strain and reserve the tea.
**2** In a juice extractor, process the papaya and then the orange until smooth. Stir in the tea.

Serves 1
Makes about 1 cup (250 ml)

# Orange Sage Juice

Sage is an anti-bacterial herb used to soothe a painful sore throat, and the vitamin C in oranges helps to prevent strep throat. Wheat germ oil contains vitamin E and essential fatty acids, while orange zest provides bioflavonoids.

2 oranges, peeled, deseeded and sliced
1 teaspoon finely chopped fresh sage
1 teaspoon grated orange zest
$1/2$ teaspoon wheat germ oil

Process the sliced orange in a juice extractor, then whisk in the remaining ingredients.

Serves 1
Makes about 1 cup (250 ml)

# Ginger Onion Carrot Drink

This spicy mix is great sinus clearer. Although strong in flavor, onion is an excellent decongestant and mucus expeller. Carrots provide beta-carotene, which helps in the repair and maintenance of mucous membranes. Ginger and wasabi both help to reduce inflammation.

$1/2$ in (1 cm) fresh ginger root, peeled and sliced
1 thin wedge onion, sliced
2 carrots, sliced
$1/4$ teaspoon wasabi paste

In a juice extractor, process the ginger, then the sliced onion and carrot until smooth. Whisk in the wasabi.

Serves 1
Makes about 1 cup (250 ml)

# Lemon Honey Drink

This drink helps to reduce bacteria in the throat and to boost the immune system. Lemon juice contains lots of vitamin C, and garlic and honey are both antibacterial foods. Horseradish helps to reduce mucus congestion.

1 clove garlic, peeled
$1/2$ lemon, peeled and sliced
$1/2$ teaspoon prepared horseradish
1–2 teaspoons honey, or to taste
$1/2$ cup (125 ml) hot water

In a juice extractor, process the garlic, then the lemon until smooth. Whisk in the horseradish, honey and hot water. Drink while hot.

Serves 1
Makes about $3/4$ cup (180 ml)

# Super Antioxidant Juice (Cancer Tonic)

This juice is not a cure, but the ingredients provide a hefty dose of antioxidants, which help rid the body of free radicals that can increase the risk of cancer.

2 medium carrots, sliced
$1/_2$ medium beetroot, sliced
1 stalk celery with leaves, sliced
$1/_2$ cup (25 g) spinach
4 sprigs fresh parsley

Process all the ingredients in a juice extractor until well blended.

Serves 1–2
Makes about $1^1/_2$ cups (375 ml)

# Apricot Orange Ginger Smoothie
## (Cholesterol Reducer)

The fiber in apricots and oat bran helps reduce cholesterol levels in the intestinal tract. Ginger, onion and garlic also help, so use plenty of these in your cooking.

5 dried apricots
$3/_4$ cup (180 ml) water
Fresh juice of 1 large orange
2 teaspoons oat bran
1 teaspoon finely grated fresh
  ginger root

1 In a small pot, bring the apricots and water to a boil. Reduce the heat to low, cover and simmer for 15 minutes. Remove from the heat and set aside to cool.
2 Combine the apricots and water with the remaining ingredients and process in a blender until smooth.

Serves 1
Makes about $1^1/_4$ cups (300 ml)

# Pear Alfalfa Heart Tonic (Cardiovascular Tonic)

This drink provides soluble fiber to help reduce cholesterol levels; vitamin E, which is an antioxidant shown to reduce cardiovascular disease; and vitamin C. The chlorophyll in the alfalfa sprouts acts as a blood tonic and internal cleanser, and garlic assists in maintaining healthy blood pressure.

1 clove garlic, peeled
1 cup (30 g) alfalfa sprouts
$1^1/_2$ pears, sliced
$1/_2$ teaspoon wheat germ oil

In a juice extractor, process the garlic, alfalfa and sliced pear until smooth, then whisk in the wheat germ oil.

Serves 1
Makes about 1 cup (250 ml)

# Blueberry Orange Cantaloupe Juice

Some essential nutrients for eye health are bioflavonoids, which help strengthen and maintain blood capillaries, and beta-carotene for its antioxidant activity, which has been shown to help reduce the incidence of cataracts and other degenerative eye disorders. Vitamin C works with bioflavonoids and is also an antioxidant.

$1/4$ medium cantaloupe (rockmelon), peeled, deseeded and sliced
1 large orange, peeled, deseeded and sliced
2 cups (250 g) fresh or thawed blueberries

Process all the ingredients in a juice extractor until well blended.

Serves 2
Makes about $1^3/_4$ cup (450 ml)

# Pineapple Ginger Juice

This drink is an excellent digestive aid. Bromelain, the enzyme in pineapple, assists in digestion, and ginger has long been used for its wind-dispelling quality.

$1/_2$ fresh medium pineapple, peeled, cored and sliced
$3/_4$ in (2 cm) fresh ginger root, peeled and sliced

Process the pineapple and ginger in a juice extractor until well blended.

Serves 1
Makes about 1 cup (250 ml)

# Apple, Pear, Beet and Ginger Juice (Eczema Aid)

The skin is an organ of elimination, and rashes can indicate the need for improved toxin removal by the body. Beets help to promote liver functions, which improves the elimination ability of the digestive system. The carotenes in beets also help to maintain good skin health. Ginger acts as an anti-inflammatory agent to help reduce the itchiness of eczema, while apple and pear provide soluble fiber.

1 apple, sliced
1 pear, sliced
$1/_2$ large beetroot, sliced
$1/_2$ in (1 cm) fresh ginger root, peeled and sliced

Process all the ingredients in a juice extractor until smooth and drink immediately.

Serves 1
Makes about 1 cup (250 ml)

# Blackberry Juice (Hemorrhoid Treater)

Pears and oat bran contain soluble fiber, which encourages elimination. Blackberries and cherries contain proanthocyanidins, which help strengthen the structure of veins. Both are important in treating hemorrhoids.

1 cup (125 g) blackberries or pitted cherries
1 medium pear, sliced
3 teaspoons oat bran

Process the blackberries and pear in a juice extractor until smooth, then whisk in the oat bran.

Serves 1
Makes about 1 cup (250 ml)

# Lemon Dandelion Artichoke Drink

This drink helps to reduce gallstone formation.

2 teaspoons roasted dandelion root
$1/4$ cup (60 ml) boiling water
$1/2$ small artichoke
1 lemon, sliced
1 in (3 cm) fresh turmeric, peeled and sliced
2 teaspoons honey, or to taste
1 teaspoon psyllium husks

1 Soak the dandelion in the boiling water and for 10 minutes. Strain, reserve the soaking liquid and chill.
2 Remove the outer leaves from the artichoke, trim the ends of the remaining leaves and cut into small pieces.
3 In a juice extractor, process the lemon, artichoke and turmeric until smooth. Combine with the dandelion soaking liquid and honey, and whisk in the psyllium.

Serves 1    Makes about 1 cup (250 ml)

# Pineapple Onion Chili Drink (Hay Fever Fighter)

Chopped onion and honey is an age-old remedy to help break up and expel mucus. Onion is a natural anti-inflammatory agent, while bromelain, the enzyme in pineapple, helps inhibit histamines, thereby reducing the allergy response.

$1/2$ large onion, finely chopped
$1/4$ cup (60 ml) honey
$1/4$ fresh medium pineapple, cored, peeled and sliced
1 small finger-length chili, sliced
$1/3$ cup (90 ml) water

1 Combine the onion and honey in a small bowl. Cover and refrigerate overnight.
2 In a juice extractor, process the pineapple and chili until smooth. Add the water and 2 teaspoons of the onion mixture and mix well. Drink immediately.

Serves 1    Makes about 1 cup (250 ml)

# Watermelon Grape Frappe

Any variety of nondairy frozen sorbet may be used in place of the strawberry.

1 cup (180 g) seedless red grapes
$1^1/_2$ cups (280 g) sliced and
deseeded watermelon
1 cup (250 ml) strawberry sorbet

Process all the ingredients in a blender until smooth.

Serves 2
Makes about $2^1/_2$ cups (625 ml)

# Green Tea Melon Frappe

This drink is very simple but utterly refreshing on a hot day. Make a strong pot of your favorite green tea, let it cool, then pour into the ice cube trays to freeze.

14 green tea ice cubes
$^1/_4$ honeydew melon, peeled,
deseeded and sliced

Allow the cubes to soften slightly, then place them in a blender with the melon and process until smooth.

Serves 2
Makes about $2^1/_2$ cups (625 ml)

# Blueberry Banana Frappe

To freeze a banana, peel it first, then seal in a plastic bag and place in the freezer for about 3 hours. Frozen banana gives this drink a creamy consistency.

1 frozen large banana, sliced
2 oranges, peeled, deseeded and
sliced
1 cup (125 g) fresh or thawed
blueberries

Process all the ingredients in a blender until smooth.

Serves 2
Makes about $2^1/_2$ cups (625 ml)

# Strawberry Peach Frappe

Fragrant fruits combine to make an ideal summertime drink.

4 oz (125 g)strawberries
2 peaches, peeled and pitted
2 plums, peeled and pitted
8 ice cubes

Process all the ingredients in a blender until smooth.

Serves 2
Makes about 2 cups (500 ml)

# Minty Melon Mix

If you have a juicer, make your own apple juice; alternatively, use a natural commercial juice. Pour the juice into ice cube trays and freeze until solid. If not using the cubes immediately, remove them from the trays and store in an airtight lock-top plastic bag to preserve their flavor. The mint adds a flavor lift to this drink, so include it if fresh mint leaves are available.

$1/4$ honeydew melon, peeled, deseeded and sliced
2 kiwifruit, peeled and sliced
8 apple juice ice cubes
3 fresh mint leaves (optional)

Process all the ingredients in a blender until smooth.

Serves 2
Makes about 2 cups (500 ml)

# Mango Peach Ginger Frappe

Mangoes and peaches are good sources of beta-carotene, a valuable antioxidant. Ginger helps to alleviate nausea. Consider taking this drink before a trip if you suffer from motion sickness. It is also a safe way to treat morning sickness.

$1/2$ in (1 cm) fresh ginger root, peeled and sliced
1 large mango, peeled and pitted
2 peaches, peeled and pitted
8 ice cubes

Process all the ingredients in a blender until smooth.

Serves 2
Makes about 2 cups (500 ml)

# Pineapple Orange Strawberry Frappe

For easy blending, it is better to allow frozen fruits to soften a bit before using. Frozen fruits make the drink quite thick. You may need to add a little water.

$1/4$ fresh pineapple, peeled, cored and sliced
4 oz (125 g) fresh or thawed strawberries
1 large orange, peeled, deseeded and sliced
8 ice cubes

Process all the ingredients in a blender until smooth.

Serves 2
Makes about $2^1/2$ cups (625 ml)

# Vegetable Crush

Red bell pepper is a good source of beta-carotene and vitamin C, and tomatoes contain the carotenoid lycopene, which may help to prevent prostate cancer. Garlic has powerful antibacterial and antiviral qualities. Celery is a good source of potassium and is a diuretic. You may like to season this drink with a little salt and pepper, or just pepper.

1 large red bell pepper, deseeded
  and sliced
1 tomato, cored and sliced
2 stalks celery, trimmed and sliced
1 small clove garlic, peeled
6 ice cubes
6 fresh basil leaves
Salt and pepper, to taste (optional)

Process all the ingredients, except the salt and pepper (if using), in a blender until smooth. Add the salt and pepper and mix well.

Serves 2
Makes about 2 cups (500 ml)

# Mango Pineapple Passion Fruit Frappe

This drink has a thick, icy consistency. Thin it with water or orange juice if preferred.

2 passion fruits, halved
1 mango, peeled and pitted
$1/2$ fresh pineapple, peeled, cored
  and sliced
8 ice cubes

Scoop out the passion fruit flesh and place in a blender. Add all the other ingredients and process until smooth.

Serves 2
Makes about 2 cups (500 ml)

# Cranberry Orange Pineapple Frappe

When peeling the orange, leave on some of the white pith containing bioflavonoids, which are antibacterial and antiviral. Cranberry juice and pineapple are good sources of vitamin C.

1 orange, peeled, deseeded and
  sliced
$1/4$ fresh pineapple, peeled, cored
  and sliced
1 cup (250 ml) cranberry juice
8 ice cubes

Process all the ingredients in a blender until smooth.

Serves 2
Makes about 2 cups (500 ml)

# Berry Citrus Blend

Berries and citrus complement one another beautifully. This drink is a nutritious blend of antioxidants in the form of bioflavonoids and vitamins. Antioxidants are believed to help in the prevention of disease and to slow physical degeneration.

$1/_2$ cup (60 g) fresh or thawed blueberries

$1/_2$ cup (60 g) fresh or thawed raspberries

2 oz (60 g) fresh or thawed straw-berries

2 large oranges, peeled and sliced

8 ice cubes

Process all the ingredients in a blender until smooth.

Serves 2
Makes about $2^1/_2$ cups (625 ml)

# Purple Passion

The purple comes from the blueberries, which contain flavonoids that promote healthy eyesight. They also help to strengthen arteries and veins.

2 passion fruits, halved

$1/_4$ fresh pineapple, peeled, cored and sliced

$1/_2$ cup (60 g) fresh or thawed frozen blueberries

8 ice cubes

Scoop out the passion fruit flesh and place in a blender. Add all the other ingredients and process until smooth.

Serves 2
Makes about 2 cups (500 ml)

# Beet Orange Grape Blend

Bottled beetroot juice is available in most supermarkets. You can also make your own juice in a juicer, using three beetroots to yield the amount required. Beetroots are a good source of folic acid, iron and calcium. The vitamin C in the orange helps the body to absorb iron. The grapes contribute antioxidants and potassium.

$1/_2$ cup (125 ml) beetroot juice

1 orange, peeled, deseeded and sliced

1 cup (125 g) seedless grapes

8 ice cubes

Process all the ingredients in a blender until smooth.

Serves 2
Makes about 2 cups (500 ml)

# Avocado Shots

In this amazingly fresh-tasting drink, cucumber, lemon and cilantro offset the creaminess of the avocado. Poured into small glasses, it is served as an aperitif. The frappe has a thick consistency. You could thin it with a little water if you like, but don't dilute too much.

Flesh from 1 small avocado
1 lemon, peeled and deseeded
1 large cucumber, peeled, deseeded and sliced
$1/3$ cup (15 g) fresh cilantro (coriander leaves)
10 ice cubes

Process all the ingredients in a blender until smooth. You may need to stop the blender, scrape down the sides of the container with a rubber spatula, then continue processing.

Serves 2–3
Makes about $2^1/2$ cups (625 ml)

# Papaya Pineapple Mango Frappe

The addition of fresh basil may seem unusual, but it adds an interesting flavor note. Basil is said to boost the immune system.

$1/4$ papaya, peeled, deseeded and sliced
$1/4$ fresh pineapple, peeled, cored and sliced
1 mango, peeled and pitted
8 ice cubes
4 fresh basil leaves (optional)

Process all the ingredients in a blender until smooth.

Serves 2
Makes about $2^1/2$ cups (625 ml)

# Papaya Banana Lime Frappe

Bananas add a creamy thickness to blended drinks. One of the most widely consumed fruits, bananas are a good source of potassium, which balances the effect of a high sodium intake and helps to regulate the heart muscle.

$1/2$ papaya, peeled, deseeded and sliced
1 banana, peeled and sliced
$1/2$ lime, peeled and deseeded
6 ice cubes

Process all the ingredients in a blender until smooth.

Serves 2
Makes about 2 cups (500 ml)

# Red Papaya Cantaloupe Frappe

Red papaya and cantaloupe are both sources of beta-carotene.
Red papaya also has lycopene, another antioxidant.

$1/2$ red papaya, peeled, deseeded
and sliced
$1/4$ cantaloupe (rockmelon),
peeled, deseeded and sliced
$1/4$ lemon, peeled and deseeded
6 ice cubes

Process all the ingredients in a blender until smooth.

Serves 1
Makes about $1 1/2$ cups (375 ml)

# Pineapple Persimmon Crush

Truly ripe Hachiya persimmons are very soft, so soft they seem almost overripe,
but this is when they taste the best. Persimmons are a good source of vitamin C,
beta-carotene and potassium.

2 ripe Hachiya persimmons
$1/4$ fresh pineapple, peeled, cored
and sliced
8 ice cubes

Cut each persimmon in half and scoop out the flesh,
discarding the seeds. Place in a blender with all the
other ingredients and process until smooth.

Serves 1
Makes about $1 1/2$ cups (375 ml)

# Tamarillo Banana Kiwifruit Frappe

Tangy tamarillos marry well with kiwifruit. They are a good source of vitamin C,
as is the kiwifruit, and of potassium, as is the banana. Choose the red-skinned
variety of tamarillos rather than the yellow for a prettier colored drink.

2 tamarillos, peeled and sliced
1 banana, peeled and sliced
2 kiwifruit, peeled and sliced
8 ice cubes

Process all the ingredients in a blender until smooth.

Serves 2
Makes about 2 cups (500 ml)

# Smoothie Soother

Both pineapple and papaya contain enzymes which aid digestion. Acidophilus yogurt helps to restore beneficial intestinal bacteria and ginger also aids digestion.

1 cup (250 ml) fresh pineapple juice
$^1/_2$ papaya, peeled, deseeded and
　sliced
1 cup (250 ml) plain yogurt
$^1/_2$ in (1 cm) fresh ginger root,
　peeled and sliced

Process all the ingredients in a blender until smooth and frothy.

Serves 2
Makes about $2^1/_2$ cups (625 ml)

# Breakfast Smoothie

If this smoothie is all you are having for breakfast, make sure not to omit the banana—it is both filling and satisfying.

1 banana, peeled and sliced
2 apricots, peeled and pitted
1 cup (250 ml) milk
2 teaspoons wheat germ
2 teaspoons oat bran
$^1/_2$ cup (125 ml) plain yogurt
2–3 teaspoons pure maple syrup
　or honey

Process all the ingredients in a blender until smooth and frothy.

Serves 2
Makes about $2^1/_2$ cups (625 ml)

# Spiced Pistachio Smoothie

This drink is reminiscent of Middle Eastern desserts. Pistachios contain monoun-saturated fat and are rich in fiber, vitamin B6, thiamin, magnesium and potassium.

$^1/_4$ cup (30 g) unsalted, shelled
　pistachios
1 cup (250 ml) milk
$^1/_2$ cup (125 ml) vanilla yogurt
Pinch of ground cardamom
Pinch of ground cinnamon
1 teaspoon sugar
Few drops rose water, or to taste
6 ice cubes

Process all the ingredients in a blender until smooth and frothy.

Serves 2
Makes about 2 cups (500 ml)

# Restorative Smoothie

This thick smoothie is great if you are trying to gain weight or build up your strength after a period of illness. The avocado provides monounsaturated fat, which helps to guard against heart disease. The Brazil nuts are a good source of selenium, an essential trace mineral that promotes growth and hormone production.

$1^1/_2$ cups (375 ml) milk
$^1/_3$ cup (90 ml) plain yogurt
1 banana, peeled and sliced
Flesh from $^1/_2$ small avocado
5 Brazil nuts
2 teaspoons honey
$^1/_2$ teaspoon grated lemon zest

Process all the ingredients in a blender until smooth and frothy.

Serves 2
Makes about 2 cups (500 ml)

# Protein Power Smoothie

Tofu is a good source of protein and calcium. It also contains some vitamin E. Make sure you buy tofu that is labeled "silken" for drink recipes.

1 cup (250 ml) milk
4 oz (125 g) silken tofu
1 banana, peeled and sliced
1 tablespoon protein whey powder
1 tablespoon carob powder
2 teaspoons brown sugar

Process all the ingredients in a blender until smooth and frothy.

Serves 2
Makes about $2^1/_2$ cups (625 ml)

# High-fiber Smoothie

Prunes have laxative qualities and are a good source of iron and potassium. Apples contain pectin, a soluble fiber. The acidophilus yogurt helps to balance the bacteria present in the intestines, making everything work smoothly.

6 pitted prunes
1 tart apple, peeled and sliced
$^1/_2$ cup (125 ml) water
1 cup (250 ml) milk
$^1/_2$ cup (125 ml) plain yogurt
1 teaspoon honey
2 teaspoons psyllium husks

**1** Bring the prunes, apple and water to a boil in a small saucepan. Reduce the heat to low, cover and simmer until very soft, about 10 minutes. Set aside to cool.
**2** Process the prunes, apple and water, with all the other ingredients in a blender until smooth and frothy.

Serves 2    Makes about $2^1/_2$ cups (625 ml)

# Strawberry Smoothie

If the strawberries lack flavor, use strawberry yogurt, preferably a naturally
flavored product, instead of the plain yogurt.

4 o (125 g) fresh or thawed strawberries
1¹/₂ cups (375 ml) milk
¹/₂ cup (125 ml) plain yogurt
Honey, to taste

Process all the ingredients in a blender until smooth
and frothy.

Serves 2–3
Makes about 3 cups (750 ml)

# Favorite Banana Smoothie

If the banana is very ripe, the smoothie may be sweet enough without the honey.
Add a couple of teaspoons of wheat germ if you like.

1 large banana, peeled and sliced
1¹/₂ cups (375 ml) milk
¹/₂ cup (125 ml) plain yogurt
Honey, to taste

Process all the ingredients in a blender until smooth
and frothy.

Serves 2
Makes about 2¹/₂ cups (625 ml)

# Banana Buttermilk Smoothie

Buttermilk, a low-fat milk product, is cultured like yogurt,
and therefore adds a delicious tang to blended drinks.

¹/₂ cup (125 ml) buttermilk
1 cup (250 ml) milk
1 large banana, peeled and sliced
1 tablespoon honey
Pinch of ground nutmeg
  or cinnamon

Process all the ingredients in a blender until smooth
and frothy.

Serves 2
Makes about 2 cups (500 ml)

# Spiced Plum Smoothie

Use three plums if they are large, or four if they are smaller.

3–4 red-fleshed plums, peeled
  and pitted
1 cup (250 ml) milk
$1/_2$ cup (125 ml) plain yogurt
Honey, to taste
Pinch of ground cinnamon
Pinch of ground cardamom

Process all the ingredients in a blender until smooth and frothy. Taste and add more cinnamon or cardamom if desired.

Serves 2
Makes about 2 cups (500 ml)

# Apricot Almond Smoothie

Almonds are a good source of vitamin E and contain mostly unsaturated fat.
Dried apricots are a rich source of beta-carotene, a valuable antioxidant.

$1/_2$ cup (90 g) dried apricots
$3/_4$ cup (180 ml) water
$1/_4$ cup (30 g) unblanched raw
  almonds
$1^1/_2$ cups (375 ml) milk

**1** In a small saucepan, bring the apricots and water to a boil. Reduce the heat to low, cover and simmer until very soft, about 10 minutes. Drain and set aside to cool.
**2** Process the apricots and water with all the other ingredients in a blender until smooth and frothy.

Serves 2
Makes about $2^1/_2$ cups (625 ml)

# Blackberry Smoothie

While it is fun to pick wild berries in the field, you need to be sure they are free
from herbicide. Blackberries are a good source of vitamin C and dietary fiber.

1 cup (125 g) fresh or thawed
  blackberries
1 cup (250 ml) milk
$1/_2$ cup (125 ml) plain or mixed
  berry yogurt
1 teaspoon grated orange zest

Process all the ingredients in a blender until smooth and frothy.

Note: For raspberry smoothie, use the same amount of raspberries in place of the blackberries.

Serves 2
Makes about 2 cups (500 ml)

# Tropical Smoothie

This cooling, tangy drink is ideal to prepare on hot days when cooking holds little appeal. Coconut milk is nutritious but is also high in fat, so choose the low-fat product whenever possible.

1 banana, peeled and sliced
$1/4$ fresh pineapple, peeled, cored and sliced
1 mango, peeled and pitted
1 cup (250 ml) coconut milk
$1/2$ cup (125 ml) mango or other tropical-fruit yogurt
4 ice cubes

Process all the ingredients in a blender until smooth and frothy.

Serves 2–3
Makes about 3 cups (750 ml)

# Fruit and Nut Smoothie

Look for yogurt which uses natural fruit flavoring with no sugar added. Alternatively, use plain yogurt and add some fresh fruit.

$1/2$ cup (90 g) golden raisins
2 tablespoons almond butter
1 cup (250 ml) milk
$1/2$ cup (125 ml) apricot yogurt or other fruit yogurt

**1** In a small bowl, soak the raisins in boiling water to cover for 5 minutes, then drain.
**2** Process the raisins with all the other ingredients in a blender until smooth and frothy.

Serves 2
Makes about 2 cups (500 ml)

# Cranberry Vanilla Smoothie

Cranberries contain vitamins C and D, as well as potassium and iron. They are effective in treating mild urinary-tract infections. The berries are quite tart, so adjust the sweetening to your taste.

1 cup (125 g) fresh or thawed cranberries
$1/2$ cup (125 ml) vanilla yogurt
1 cup (250 ml) milk
2 teaspoons honey, or to taste

Process all the ingredients in a blender until smooth and frothy.

Serves 2
Makes about 2 cups (500 ml)

# Summertime Blend

If you are using frozen raspberries, allow them to soften a little but not thaw completely. The cold berries will add a welcome chill to the drink. You may want to add a couple of ice cubes if you are using fresh raspberries.

2 peaches, peeled and pitted
1 cup (125 g) fresh or thawed
  raspberries
1 cup (250 ml) milk
1/2 cup (125 ml) plain yogurt
2 teaspoons honey, or to taste

Process all the ingredients in a blender until smooth and frothy.

Serves 2
Makes about 2 1/2 cups (625 ml)

# Fruit Salad Smoothie

Using a frozen banana gives this drink a thick, creamy consistency, but it will be equally delicious with a fresh banana. Bananas are difficult to peel once they are frozen, so peel the banana first, then seal in a plastic bag with the air expelled before placing in the refrigerator. It will take about 3 hours for the banana to freeze.

1/2 cup (60 g) fresh or thawed
  strawberries
1 frozen banana, sliced
2 nectarines, pitted
1/2 cup (125 ml) fresh orange juice
1/2 cup (125 ml) vanilla yogurt

Process all the ingredients in a blender until smooth and frothy.

Serves 2
Makes about 2 1/2 cups (625 ml)

# Berry Apple Smoothie

If you are fortunate to have access to a mulberry tree, then make the most of the short mulberry season by preparing this delicious drink. Other berries in season, such as loganberries or boysenberries, may be substituted.

1 tart apple, peeled, cored and
  sliced
1 cup (125 g) mulberries
1/2 cup (125 ml) vanilla yogurt
1 cup (250 ml) milk

Steam the apple in a steamer over boiling water until very soft, about 5 minutes. Process the apple and all the other ingredients in a blender until smooth and frothy.

Serves 2
Makes about 2 cups (500 ml)

# Cherry Berry Smoothie

Pitting cherries may seem laborious, but using a cherry pitter makes the task quick and easy. Cherries are a good source of potassium and are believed to help in the prevention and treatment of gout, a type of arthritis.

$1/_2$ cup (75 g) sweet cherries, pitted
4 oz (125 g) fresh or thawed
  strawberries
1 cup (250 ml) milk
$1/_2$ cup (125 ml) plain yogurt
1 teaspoon honey or maple syrup,
  or to taste

Process all the ingredients in a blender until smooth and frothy.

Serves 2
Makes about $2^1/_2$ cups (625 ml)

# Berry Shake

Frozen yogurt is a tasty alternative to ice cream, and low-fat varieties are available. Regular yogurt can also be used.

4 oz (125 g) fresh or thawed
  strawberries
1 cup (250 ml) milk
1 cup (250 ml) mixed berry frozen
  yogurt
Honey, to taste

Process all the ingredients in a blender until smooth and frothy.

Serves 2
Makes about $2^1/_2$ cups (625 ml)

# Banana Date Smoothie

For this smoothie, use the semi-dry dates, which are softer and have a higher moisture content. If only dried dates are available, cook them in $3/_4$ cup (180 ml) of water for 10 minutes.

4 semi-dry dates, pitted and
  chopped
$1/_3$ cup (90 ml) water
1 banana, peeled and sliced
1 cup (250 ml) milk
$1/_2$ cup (125 ml) plain yogurt
Pinch of ground nutmeg

1 In a small saucepan, bring the dates and water to a boil, then reduce the heat to low, cover and simmer until the dates are soft, about 3 minutes. Drain and set aside to cool completely.
2 Process the dates and all the other ingredients in a blender until smooth and frothy.

Serves 2    Makes about $2^1/_2$ cups (625 ml)

# Strawberry Soy Shake

Silken tofu is the best type to use in drinks, as firmer tofu will not blend to a nice smooth texture. Silken tofu is quite fragile and easily falls apart when handled.

1 cup (250 ml) soy milk
4 oz (125 g) silken tofu
4 oz (125 g) fresh or thawed
  strawberries
1–2 tablespoons honey

Process all the ingredients in a blender until smooth and frothy.

Serves 2
Makes about $2^1/_2$ cups (625 ml)

# Orange Peach Smoothie

Peaches are easily digestible fruits that contain vitamins A and C, both of which are antioxidants.

1 cup (250 ml) fresh orange juice
2 peaches, peeled and pitted
$1/_2$ cup (125 ml) peach soy yogurt

Process all the ingredients in a blender until smooth and frothy.

Serves 2
Makes about $2^1/_2$ cups (625 ml)

# Mango Oat Milk Shake

Cashews are a good source of protein and also contain calcium, magnesium and vitamins B1 and B2. They are high in unsaturated fat, which may assist in the prevention of heart disease.

1 cup (250 ml) oat milk
1 mango, peeled and pitted
$1/_4$ cup (30 g) raw cashews
$1/_2$ cup (125 ml) tropical fruit
  sorbet

Process all the ingredients in a blender until smooth and frothy.

Serves 2
Makes about $2^1/_2$ cups (625 ml)

# Iced Soy Latte

For a mocha variation, add 1 tablespoon cocoa powder when dissolving the coffee. You may also need to add a little bit more water.

1 teaspoon instant coffee powder
  or granules
1 tablespoon boiling water
1¹/₂ cups (375 ml) soy milk
1 cup (250 ml) vanilla soy ice
  cream

In a small bowl, dissolve the coffee powder in boiling water and allow to cool, then process in a blender with all the other ingredients until frothy.

Serves 2
Makes about 2¹/₂ cups (625 ml)

# Custard Apple Shake

Custard apples, also known as cherimoyas, have a creamy consistency and a subtle but refreshing flavor. They are a good source of vitamin C and potassium.

1 custard apple (about 180 g)
1 peach, peeled and pitted
1 cup (250 ml) rice milk
³/₄ cup (180 ml) vanilla soy ice
  cream
Pinch of ground nutmeg

Cut the custard apple in half and scoop out the flesh, discarding the seeds. Process the custard apple flesh with all the other ingredients in a blender until smooth and frothy.

Serves 2
Makes about 2¹/₂ cups (625 ml)

# Muesli Mix Shake

This drink makes a great breakfast when you are on the go. The dried fruits and nuts provide energy and fiber, and wheat germ is a good source of vitamins.

¹/₄ cup (45 g) dried apricots
¹/₄ cup (25 g) dried apples
³/₄ cup (180 ml) water
1 cup (250 ml) oat milk
¹/₄ cup (45 g) unblanched raw
  almonds
¹/₂ cup (125 ml) vanilla soy yogurt
2 teaspoons wheat germ

**1** In a small saucepan, bring the apricots, apples and water to a boil. Reduce the heat to low, cover and simmer until the fruits are very soft, about 10 minutes. Remove from the heat, drain and set aside to cool.
**2** Process the fruits with all the other ingredients in a blender until smooth and frothy.

Serves 2
Makes about 2 cups (500 ml)

# Cantaloupe Crush

You may also freeze the cantaloupe well in advance of preparing the crush, then thaw it partially before using. The texture of the semi-frozen fruit gives the drink a thick, icy consistency.

$1/_4$ cantaloupe (rockmelon), peeled, deseeded and cubed
1 cup (250 ml) vanilla soy yogurt
$1/_2$ cup (125 ml) fresh orange juice

Place the cantaloupe cubes in a freezer bag, seal and freeze until partially frozen, about 1 hour. Process the partially frozen cantaloupe and all the other ingredients in a blender until smooth and frothy.

Serves 2
Makes about 2 cups (500 ml)

# Pineapple Coconut Whip

Pineapples are very refreshing fruits that are a good source of vitamin C and fiber. They also contain the enzyme bromelain, which works to break down proteins, making it a digestive aid. Only fresh pineapples contain bromelain, as it is destroyed in the process of canning.

$1/_4$ fresh pineapple, peeled, cored and sliced
1 cup (250 ml) tropical fruit sorbet
1 banana, peeled and sliced
$1^1/_2$ tablespoons unsweetened shredded dried coconut
8 ice cubes

Process all the ingredients in a blender until smooth and frothy.

Serves 2
Makes about $2^1/_2$ cups (625 ml)

# Banana Raisin Nut Blend

Macadamias are high in calories and, monounsaturated fat, which is believed to reduce blood cholesterol levels. They are also rich in protein and potassium.

$1/_3$ cup (60 g) golden raisin
$1^1/_2$ cups (375 ml) rice milk
1 banana, peeled and sliced
$1/_3$ cup (45 g) raw macadamia nuts

In a small bowl, soak the raisins in boiling water for 5 minutes, then drain. Process the raisins and all the other ingredients in a blender until smooth and frothy.

Serves 2    Makes about $2^1/_2$ cups (625 ml)

# Mocha Latte Shake

Coffee and chocolate, known as mocha, is a delicious flavor combination. This is a drink for adults, as children should not consume caffeine.

1 teaspoon instant coffee powder
  or granules
1 tablespoon boiling water
$1^1/_2$ cups (375 ml) milk
1 cup (250 ml) vanilla or chocolate
  ice cream
1 tablespoon chocolate syrup
Sweetened cocoa powder,
  to serve

In a small bowl, dissolve the coffee powder in boiling water and allow to cool. Briefly pulse the dissolved coffee in a blender with the milk, ice cream and syrup until frothy. Pour into serving glasses, dust with the cocoa powder and serve.

Serves 2
Makes about $2^1/_2$ cups (625 ml)

# Caramel Milk Shake

Look for a good-quality caramel syrup. It can also be used as a sauce on ice cream, fruit and other desserts. You can add a banana to this drink, which not only increases its nutritional value but makes it absolutely delicious.

$1^1/_2$ cups (375 ml) milk
1 cup (250 ml) vanilla ice cream
2 tablespoons caramel syrup

Process all the ingredients in a blender until smooth and frothy.

Serves 2
Makes about $2^1/_2$ cups (625 ml)

# Chocolate Orange Shake

Orange sorbet may be used in place of the ice cream and orange zest. The zest adds to the intensity of the orange flavor, however, you can still include it if you like.

$1^1/_2$ cups (375 ml) milk
1 cup (250 ml) vanilla ice cream
1 tablespoon chocolate syrup
1 teaspoon finely grated orange
  zest

Process all the ingredients in a blender until smooth and frothy.

Serves 2
Makes about $2^1/_2$ cups (625 ml)

# Berry Yogurt Shake

You can use only one type of berry or use a combination of different types.

1 cup (250 ml) milk
1 cup (250 ml) mixed berry yogurt
1 cup (250 ml) vanilla ice cream
1 cup (60 g) fresh or thawed blueberries, or raspberries, or $1/2$ cup
  (30 g) of each

Process all the ingredients in a blender until smooth
and frothy.

Serves 3
Makes about $3^1/_2$ cups (875 ml)

# Banana Split Shake

This drink has all the flavors of a banana split blended together and served in a
glass. Choose a peanut butter without added salt or sugar.

$1^1/_2$ cups (375 ml) milk
1 tablespoon peanut butter
1 cup (250 ml) vanilla ice cream
1 tablespoon chocolate syrup
1 banana, peeled and sliced

Process all the ingredients in a blender until smooth
and frothy.

Serves 2
Makes about $2^1/_2$ cups (625 ml)

# Mango Milk Shake

Sorbet is virtually fat free. If you make this shake with low-fat milk, it is quite a
healthy drink—with the bonus of beta-carotene and vitamin C from the mango.

$1^1/_2$ cups (375 ml) milk
1 mango, peeled and pitted, then
  sliced
$1/_2$ cup (125 ml) tropical fruit
  sorbet

Process all the ingredients in a blender until smooth
and frothy.

Serves 2
Makes about $2^1/_2$ cups (625 ml)

# Chocolate Milk Shake

Choose a high-quality brand of ice cream that will give the shake a creamy rather than icy texture. You could use chocolate ice cream to intensify the flavor if you like.

1¹/₂ cups (375 ml) milk
1 cup (250 ml) vanilla ice cream
2 tablespoons chocolate syrup
1 teaspoon finely grated milk
  chocolate (optional)

Process all the ingredients, except the milk chocolate, in a blender until frothy. Pour into serving glasses and sprinkle the grated milk chocolate on top.

Serves 2
Makes about 2¹/₂ cups (625 ml)

# Caramel Date Milk Shake

This drink is very sweet from the natural sugars in the dates as well as the caramel syrup. The flavor combination is divine, but you may like to tone it down by adding a little more milk, according to your taste.

4 semi-dry dates, pitted and chopped
¹/₃ cup (90 ml) water
1¹/₂ cups (375 ml) milk
1 cup (250 ml) vanilla ice cream
1 tablespoon caramel syrup
Pinch of ground nutmeg
Pinch of ground cinnamon

1 In a small saucepan, bring the dates and water to a boil. Reduce the heat to low, cover and simmer until the dates are soft, about 3 minutes. Set aside to cool.
2 Process the dates and water together with all the other ingredients in a blender until smooth and frothy.

Serves 2–3
Makes about 3 cups (750 ml)

# Honey Macadamia Shake

Toasting the macadamia nuts is advisable as it seems to accentuate their flavor. Like most nuts, macadamias are a good source of unsaturated fat, which helps to reduce blood cholesterol.

¹/₂ cup (75 g) macadamia nuts
1¹/₂ cups (375 ml) milk
1 cup (250 ml) vanilla ice cream
1 tablespoon honey

Serves 2
Makes about 2¹/₂ cups (625 ml)

1 Preheat the oven to 350 °F (180 °C). Spread the nuts on a baking sheet and bake until fragrant and lightly toasted, about 5 minutes. Set aside to cool, then coarsely chop the nuts.
2 Process the chopped nut with all the other ingredients in a blender until smooth and frothy.

# Orange Sherbet Shake

Orange may seem like an unusual flavor for a milk shake, but it is delicious. The zest contains oils that carry the intensely aromatic orange flavor.

2 teaspoons finely grated orange
  zest
1 cup (250 ml) fresh orange juice,
  chilled
$1/2$ cup (125 ml) milk
1 cup (250 ml) vanilla ice cream

Process all the ingredients in a blender until smooth and frothy.

Serves 2
Makes about $2^1/_2$ cups (625 ml)

# Vanilla Malted Milk Shake

This shake is a classic. Malt is derived from barley and is sold as either liquid malt or malted milk powder. The liquid is a thick brown syrup that contains phosphorus and magnesium, and the powder is dried malt combined with dried milk. Both are fortifying, nutritious products.

$1^1/_2$ cups (375 ml) milk
1 cup (250 ml) vanilla ice cream
Dash of vanilla extract
1 tablespoon malted milk powder
  or liquid malt

Process all the ingredients in a blender until smooth and frothy.

Serves 2
Makes about $2^1/_2$ cups (625 ml)

# Iced Coffee Shake

For this drink, brew your own coffee, as the intense coffee flavor is essential. True coffee aficionados will grind their own beans, but as long as you begin with good purchased ground coffee, prepared correctly, that will suffice.

2 cups (500 ml) freshly brewed
  coffee, chilled
2 cups (500 ml) vanilla ice cream
Pinch of ground cinnamon
Sugar, to taste

Briefly process the coffee, ice cream and cinnamon in a blender until frothy, then add the sugar (if using) and stir until the sugar is dissolved

Serves 4
Makes about 4 cups (1 liter)

# Chocolate Cherry Coconut Shake

Fresh cherries have a short season, so you can use frozen or canned cherries if necessary. Grate the chocolate on the finest rasps of a grater.

2 oz (60 g) dark chocolate, grated
1 cup (250 ml) low-fat coconut milk
1 cup (250 ml) vanilla ice cream
$^1/_2$ cup (75 g) fresh, frozen or
  canned sweet cherries, pitted
1 teaspoon finely grated dark
  chocolate, to serve (optional)

Process all the ingredients, except the dark chocolate for serving, in a blender until frothy. Pour into serving glasses and sprinkle the grated dark chocolate on top, if using.

Serves 2
Makes about 2 cups (500 ml)

# Mango Toasted Coconut Shake

This thick, creamy drink makes a cool treat on a hot summer day.

2 tablespoons unsweetened
  shredded dried coconut
2 mangoes, peeled and pitted
1 cup (250 ml) mango sorbet
1 cup (250 ml) vanilla ice cream
$^1/_2$ cup (125 ml) milk

**1** Dry-roast the coconut in a skillet over medium heat, stirring constantly, until golden. Remove from the heat and set aside to cool.
**2** Process all the ingredients in a blender until smooth and frothy.

Serves 2     Makes about $2^1/_2$ cups (625 ml)

# Warm Banana Chocolate Float

This delicious drink is worth the effort.

2 bananas
3 oz (90 g) milk chocolate, broken
  into pieces
$1^1/_2$ cups (375 ml) milk
2 scoops vanilla ice cream

Serves 2
Makes about $2^1/_2$ cups (625 ml)

**1** Preheat the oven to 350 °F (180 °C).
**2** Peel the bananas and cut them in half lengthwise. Place the banana halves on a sheet of aluminum foil and arrange the chocolate pieces on top. Mold the foil around the banana so the chocolate remains on top and crimp the foil to form a parcel. Place the parcel on a baking sheet and bake in the oven for 15 minutes.
**3** Heat the milk in a saucepan over medium heat until hot but not boiling. Briefly pulse the banana with chocolate in a blender, then add the heated milk and process until frothy. Serve in individual serving glasses or mugs, topping each with a scoop of ice cream.

# Peaches Cream Shake

This shake demands perfectly ripe fresh peaches. It can also be made
with canned peaches when not in season.

2 peaches, peeled and pitted,
  or 4 canned peach halves
$1/_2$ cup (125 ml) natural peach
  juice or juice from canned peaches
$1/_2$ cup (125 ml) milk
1 cup (250 ml) vanilla ice cream
Pinch of ground cinnamon or
  nutmeg, or both

Process all the ingredients in a blender until smooth
and frothy.

Serves 2
Makes about $2^1/_2$ cups (625 ml)

# Praline Shake

$1/_2$ cup (20 g) sliced almonds
$1/_2$ cup (60 g) superfine (caster)
  sugar
1 tablespoon water
1 cup (250 ml) milk
1 cup (250 ml) vanilla ice cream

Serves 2
Makes about $2^1/_4$ cups (575 ml)

1 Line a baking sheet with aluminum foil and lightly
grease it. Place the sliced almond on the foil close
together in a single layer.
2 In a small saucepan, heat the sugar and water over
medium heat and stir until the sugar is dissolved, about
5 minutes. Remove from the heat. Carefully pour the
syrup over the almonds and set aside to cool. When
the Praline is cold and hard, after about 5 minutes, break
it into pieces and process in a food processor until fine.
3 Process $1/_2$ of the ground Praline with the milk and
ice cream in a blender until smooth and frothy.

# Butterscotch Pecan Shake

It is worth the effort to make your own butterscotch sauce. In a pinch, you
could use a commercial sauce; choose a good quality brand for the best flavor.

1 tablespoon butter
2 tablespoons heavy cream
1 tablespoon brown sugar
Few drops vanilla extract
$1/_4$ cup (30 g) pecans
1 cup (250 ml) milk
1 cup (250 ml) vanilla ice cream

1 In a small saucepan, heat the butter, cream and
sugar over low heat and stir until the sugar is dissolved
and the mixture is smooth. Stir in the vanilla, remove
from the heat and set aside to cool.
2 Process the butterscotch mixture and all the other
ingredients in a blender until smooth and frothy.

Serves 2    Makes about $2^1/_4$ cups (575 ml)

# Blueberry Cheesecake Shake

The flavors of classic blueberry cheesecake are faithfully reproduced here. Even without using low-fat milk, the shake is still lower in fat than a slice of cheesecake.

1 cup (250 ml) milk
1/3 cup (90 ml) soft cream cheese
1 cup (125 g) fresh or thawed
　blueberries
1 teaspoon icing sugar
1 teaspoon finely grated lemon zest
Few drops vanilla extract

Process all the ingredients in a blender until smooth and frothy.

Serves 2
Makes about 2 1/2 cups (625 ml)

# Apples à La Mode

This has all the appeal of a good apple pie and none of the bother of making pastry.

2 tart apples, peeled, cored and
　sliced
1 cup (250 ml) milk
1/2 cup (125 ml) vanilla ice cream
1 teaspoon brown sugar
Pinch of ground cinnamon

**1** Steam the sliced apple in a steamer over boiling water until very soft, about 5 minutes. Remove from the heat and set aside to cool.
**2** Process the apple and all the other ingredients in a blender until smooth and frothy.

Serves 2
Makes about 2 cups (500 ml)

# Tiramisu Shake

Mascarpone, an ingredient in the Italian dessert tiramisu, is an Italian fresh cheese with a thick, creamy consistency and a slightly tangy flavor. This drink is delicious with ladyfingers, another component of the Italian dessert. Feel free to dunk them in the drink.

1 cup (250 ml) milk
1/2 cup (125 g) mascarpone
3 teaspoons superfine (caster) sugar
2 tablespoons cold strong black
　coffee
Sweetened cocoa, to serve

Process all the ingredients, except the cocoa, in a blender until smooth and frothy. Pour into serving glasses and dust with the cocoa.

Serves 1–2
Makes about 1 3/4 cups (450 ml)

# Espresso Freeze

For this drink, you will need a blender that can process ice cubes.
Use a good quality coffee and serve the drink in little glasses after dinner.
The recipe may be doubled to serve four without overloading the blender.

1 cup (250 ml) strong black coffee
2 tablespoons condensed milk
Pinch of ground cinnamon
Few drops vanilla extract

Serves 1
Makes about 1 cup (250 ml)

**1** Let the coffee cool, then pour into ice cube trays and freeze until solid in the freezer.
**2** Place the frozen coffee cubes in a blender and pulse in short bursts until grainy. Add all the other ingredients and process until well combined. Spoon into small chilled glasses and serve immediately, accompanied with small spoons.

# Crème Caramel Shake

Look for prepared custard in cartons in the refrigerator section of supermarkets.
Reduced-fat varieties are available, and because of the thick consistency,
you can barely tell the difference.

1 cup (250 ml) chilled vanilla custard
$1/2$ cup (125 ml) milk
1 cup (250 ml) vanilla ice cream
2 teaspoons caramel syrup,
   or to taste

Process all the ingredients in a blender until smooth and frothy.

Serves 2
Makes about $2^1/2$ cups (625 ml)

# Black Forest Shake

The inspiration for this drink is the famous Black Forest cake, a delicious
chocolate cake with a Morello cherry filling. Morello cherries are sometimes
called tart, or sour, cherries. They are not edible raw but, bottled in syrup,
have a distinctive tang. Make sure that the cherries are all pitted before using.

$1^1/2$ cups (375 ml) milk
1 cup (250 ml) chocolate ice cream
$1/2$ cup (90 g) drained bottled
   Morello cherries
1 tablespoon chocolate syrup

Process all the ingredients in a blender until smooth and frothy.

Serves 2
Makes about $2^1/2$ cups (625 ml)

# Warm Marshmallow Bliss

This drink can also be made with dark chocolate, but the white chocolate has a distinctive flavor that marries well with marshmallows.

1 1/2 cups (375 ml) milk
3/4 cup (90 g) white chocolate
1/2 cup (30 g) coarsely chopped white marshmallow
Sweetened cocoa powder, to serve

Serves 2
Makes about 2 cups (500 ml)

1 In a small saucepan, heat the milk until hot but not boiling and remove from the heat. Chop the white chocolate and add it to the saucepan with the marshmallow, stirring until they begin to soften and dissolve.
2 Warm the blender container by filling it with hot water, then emptying it. Pour the milk mixture into the blender and process until smooth and frothy. Serve in thick glasses or mugs, dusting with the cocoa powder.

# Rhubarb Smoothie

Rhubarb is very tart and requires sugar to make it palatable. Rhubarb contains calcium, potassium and thiamin. Make sure you discard the leaves, which are toxic.

2 stalks rhubarb, trimmed and cut into 1-in (3-cm) pieces
2 tablespoons water
1 tablespoon brown sugar
1 in (3 cm) cinnamon stick
1 cup (250 ml) fresh orange juice
1/2 cup (125 ml) vanilla yogurt

1 Combine the rhubarb, water, sugar and cinnamon in a saucepan. Cover and cook over low heat until the rhubarb is very soft, about 10 minutes. Cool the mixture completely, then discard the cinnamon stick.
2 Process the rhubarb mixture with all the other ingredients in a blender until smooth.

Serves 2    Makes about 2 1/2 cups (625 ml)

# Creamy Mandarin Shake

Star anise has a mild anise flavor, whereas cardamom has an intense, slightly citrus like fragrance. Rosewater, used in Middle Eastern desserts, has a lovely sweet perfume. Any of these additions enhance this drink, but it is also good without them.

3 mandarin oranges
1 cup (250 ml) vanilla ice cream
1 cup (250 ml) milk
Pinch of ground star anise or cardamom, or a few drops rose water (optional)

Peeled, deseed and slice the mandarin oranges. Then, process all the ingredients in a blender until smooth and frothy.

Serves 2
Makes about 2 1/2 cups (625 ml)

# Strawberry Daiquiri

It is best to make this drink when strawberries are at the peak of their season and are sweet, ripe and juicy. Use frozen strawberries if you know they are good quality.

8 oz (250 g) fresh or thawed
 strawberries
12 ice cubes

Process all the ingredients in a blender until smooth and frothy.

Serves 2
Makes about $2^1/_2$ cups (625 ml)

# Chilled Eggnog

Eggnog doesn't always have to be warm, as this tasty drink proves. If you are serving this drink for a special occasion, make your own custard using a vanilla bean. Otherwise, use prepared custard, sold in cartons in the refrigerator section of supermarkets.

1 cup (250 ml) chilled vanilla
 custard
$1/_2$ cup (125 ml) milk
1 cup (250 ml) vanilla ice cream
Ground nutmeg, to serve

Process all the ingredients, except the nutmeg, in a blender until smooth and frothy. Pour into serving glasses and dust with the ground nutmeg.

Serves 2
Makes about $2^1/_2$ cups (625 ml)

# Banana Blitz

Reminiscent of a piña colada, this drink is thickened with banana and has a lovely pineapple flavor. To make the pineapple ice cubes, pour pineapple juice into ice cube trays and freeze until solid. If you don't have time to make the ice cubes, double the juice and use ice cubes made with water.

1 large banana, peeled and sliced
8 pineapple juice ice cubes
$1/_2$ cup (125 ml) fresh pineapple
 juice
$1/_2$ cup (125 ml) low-fat coconut
 milk

Process all the ingredients in a blender until smooth and frothy.

Serves 2
Makes about $2^1/_2$ cups (625 ml)

# Spicy Mary

This drink is great to make in summer when tomatoes are at their peak.
Serve before dinner with appropriate hors d'oeuvres.

1 lb (500 g) ripe tomatoes
$1/_2$ lemon, deseeded and sliced
1 teaspoon Worcestershire sauce
Few drops Tabasco, or to taste
4 ice cubes
Salt and freshly ground black
  pepper, to taste

Process all the ingredients, except the salt and pepper, in a blender until smooth, then season with the salt and pepper.

Serves 2–3
Makes about 3 cups (750 ml)

# Mint Tea Slush

Because this recipe calls for a relatively large quantity of frozen tea, you could freeze it in a small, shallow metal or plastic pan rather than in ice cube trays.

2 cups (500 ml) strong black tea,
  frozen
$1/_2$ cup (125 ml) strong tea, chilled
2 tablespoons fresh mint leaves,
  coarsely chopped
1 tablespoon sugar, or to taste

Allow the frozen tea to soften slightly. If the frozen tea is in one piece rather than ice cubes, break it up into smaller pieces. Process the frozen tea with all the other ingredients in a blender until smooth yet icy.

Serves 2
Makes about $2^1/_2$ cups (625 ml)

# Coffee Shake

Experiment with different flavors of brewed coffee for this one.

1 cup (250 ml) milk
2 cups (500 ml) chocolate ice
  cream
3 tablespoons brewed coffee
Pinch of ground cinnamon
  (optional)
Sweetened cocoa, to serve

Process all the ingredients, except the cocoa, in a blender until smooth and frothy. Pour into serving glasses and dust with the cocoa.

Serves 2–3
Makes about 3 cups (750 ml)

# Complete List of Recipes